what if red ran out

Katia Grubisic

What if red ran out

Copyright © 2008 by Katia Grubisic.

All rights reserved. No part of this work may be reproduced or used in any form or by any means, electronic or mechanical, including photocopying, recording, or any retrieval system, without the prior written permission of the publisher or a licence from the Canadian Copyright Licensing Agency (Access Copyright). To contact Access Copyright, visit www.accesscopyright.ca or call 1-800-893-5777.

Edited by Karen Solie.
Cover: *Red Ink Water Abstract* © Clavusherzlinde545 | Dreamstime.com.
Cover and interior design by Julie Scriver.
Printed in Canada on 100% PCW paper.
10 9 8 7 6 5 4 3 2 1

Library and Archives Canada Cataloguing in Publication

Grubisic, Katia
What if red ran out / Katia Grubisic.

Poems.
ISBN 978-0-86492-509-1

I. Title.
PS8613.R83W43 2008   C811'.6   C2007-907353-0

Goose Lane Editions acknowledges the financial support of the Canada Council for the Arts, the Government of Canada through the Book Publishing Industry Development Program (BPIDP), and the New Brunswick Department of Wellness, Culture and Sport for its publishing activities.

Goose Lane Editions
Suite 330, 500 Beaverbrook Court
Fredericton, New Brunswick
CANADA E3B 5X4
www.gooselane.com

> A crowd
> Will gather, and not know it walks the very street
> Whereon a thing once walked that seemed a burning cloud.
> — W.B. Yeats

> La nuit est noire, la nuit
> est noire.

Contents

I

11 Wayfarer
13 Before Its Time
15 A List Before Departure
16 Baffled King Collage
17 Loose Rope Tantrum
18 The Audubon Guide to Self-Pity
19 Raven on the Watertower
20 A Hyena at the Bodega
21 Conservatory
22 With Arms Outstretched on the Lambton Line
24 On the Eve of Return to Hamelin
26 Prelude to Jumping in the River
27 Talking like Stones in the Night Zoo

II

31 Preemptive Fieldnotes

III

41 Taking Apart the Harbour
43 Paradise, Dam, North Shore
44 On the floating dock, silvered
45 When the Ice Breaks
46 Poem for the Sand Verbena Moth
47 Basin No. 3

48 Oversight
49 Warm Water Train
51 Ship in a Bottle
52 The Rough Guide to Home
54 Manifesto for August
58 Song of my Old Lead Pipes
59 Ladder to the Middle

IV

63 Barometer
65 Life Jacket
66 Strawberry Jam
68 En promenant ma peine d'amour
69 Crash Cymbal
71 The Time of Figs
74 Sun Days
75 Errand
76 Silk Pouch Hardware
78 Last Tango in Outremont
79 Utensils after the Inquisition
80 Never More Temperate
81 Love Song for the End of the World
82 To take away, or be slowly taken

85 *Notes*

I

Wayfarer

> "Traitement de cauchemars, hôpital Sacré-Cœur"
> "have you seen my keys?"
> — *posted on construction-site plywood*

He dreams he is the world, he understands
the constitution of flesh, briefly, fleetingly, as such flashes go. The quiet

is a bottoming out, a shock to his busy heart. In the dream,
from which he knows no idea should solidify,

a bus growls, an icicle sighs from a wire, a wolf
rattles by. If there are two wolves, that's fine. When it turns

sour, he marvels at the unseen killer's face. Even with the filmy tuck
of a blanket over his agitation, he is unable to stop

talking in his sleep. The whole place smells
bearish: sacred, rancid and serrated. No one ever sees it

coming. There are parts that relent
a little. How much is he hoping for? Sometimes hope

hurts more. It gives no account of itself, sits there cross-legged hinting
that every day will be the last. Some doors

won't materialize and don't go anywhere
special, and he speaks his silent

goodbyes among sudden, inexplicable willow roots.
He opens his mouth wide enough to betray

himself, get rid of those lesser
disclosures aloud. The waking self

eventually stops responding, waits for him to finish
tracing the outside shore

with whomever — maybe a known companion
who holds others' breath

in her own lungs, jealously parsing it
over the winter months. Whatever comes next

will remain unfinished.

Before Its Time

It began with an elegy for a goldfish and the list went on
to include the practice
of entomological Buddhism; also
do a bit of laundry. Worry less
about feverish urges. Though the rules
stipulate that domesticated animals
other than fish do not qualify as nature,
I roamed the house through my lens. Clicked a wall
about to wrap its arms around itself in consolation,
well-documented mural behaviour. They tend to embrace,
drop back and forth and roll
into the shape of a well, deep and endlessly
plumbable, though not always yielding
coins and pitched girls.

About that jungle I lived in — you should have seen
the fish's barely suppressed drapetomania: no matter
where you'd put it, it would remain
inoperably dissatisfied. No way
to hold it, shuttered
in 35-millimetre reams
nor with the business end of a Bowie knife,
slit carefully to the organ
that triggers the meagre packing of a satchel
on a stick. See, it longed to be montivagant,
to conquer every peak known to fish,
to earn a sponsorship from Cheerios or Adidas,
only to find that what's longed for
whether held or beheld
like two birds in the bush is the result
of the proverbs in our veins and fins.
You might think that anything kept

in water for so long could sprout rootlets and be planted at last
    grow into a new category. Naturally
there is no respite
from these urges, nor from the bugs whose bloody abdomens
I cleaned off my arms and off the glass, like quivering
fishnet stockings. I had all these holes chomped
in my person, evoked a woodcut — Woman in Someone Else's
Menagerie — displayed in a big house
not mine, with a front door that wouldn't open. It smelled
feral to me, cross-legged
on a stool with Seamus in my lap
as he had been in an old-world bookstore, but he was a whole
different species then, from an earlier volume including
bicycle (stolen), flea market sweater (grimly detested
by my mother-in-law); including youth and its attendant
wonder at formalism. Now a grey tabby
with a more phagocentric interest in skunks.

Meanwhile outside these birds — named apparently
chickadee and female downy woodpecker —
are not officially domesticated, though they eat from the feeder, know
me and the rattle of the seed bucket. So is it recognition
that makes us return, or stay? The tacit agreement not to eat
each other, to do more than pick
at scabs and watch for the unlikely
eight-year-old goldfish to die, writing an elegy
before its time after its time
should have been.

A List Before Departure

I will put all my clothes in boxes, address them to myself
with old-fashioned labels, perhaps forget

to keep any for the journey. I will dismantle the room
for broken chairs with great potential,

fished out of the garbage, but leave untouched the cellar.
In building the house, I made a place for looking

glasses, one for art, a room for piles of fire. The stoneware lamp,
traded from the junk man for two wiggly-glassed windows,

I will bring to light the way, plug trailing. I will leave
the flour, the frozen butter awaiting

transformation, the rolled oats.
I do not wish to build for a time.

This is what it looks like to run away from home, mantled
with lichens from crawling through the old soft fences

of Ontario border farms. Like others
who have successfully lost their minds, I will exist

on raspberries, thieve new eggs from nests, and find
my night fears quelled by gentler rural bogeymen, their absence.

Baffled King Collage

What if the things we fear are
Leonard Cohen covers, or
coats made of chagrin,
well worn and unintentionally
the right size; what if
a peculiar scarcity
of bell tollers left
coppery gothic whistles stunning
the city; what if
red ran out; what if it ends up
you and me and another
hallelujah, not much godly
about it; and those slit cardboard eclipse thingies
are no good
and we are condemned
to suffer a dreadful fate,
ambling around half blind
in this coat we hadn't anticipated.
Unwilling to toss it
casually as if we did this
all the time, over the lone, lonely tree,
in case its branches refuse
to bend as much as we want.

Loose Rope Tantrum

Look at him bouncing insistently
like a solitary god, unable to apprehend
the northern lights with his camera. Of course
gods have cameras; though divine photojournalism
has a ways to go, there are plenty of not bad
drawn-out long shots — railroads, pipes, a wire
with the guy balancing, trying to make it
from one rooftop to another.
He has things to say, wants a sky
to say them from. He's no Mary Poppins
but the rope will take his weight. It gives,
welcomes even as he steps forward with aplomb
and unleaden feet, the back-light rendering
him a cliché: warped, melancholy, magnetic.

The Audubon Guide to Self-Pity

When I lost the taste
for robins, I began taking pictures
of red. Maybe I was part
hummingbird (had my parents
made out in the back
of a corolla?). How do you replace
that firm grasp on a body,
the familiarity of the hunt? I lost
the bridge, its haunched
girders curving like the charm
of talons, the river's
rusty tang and the impossibility
of running the other way. In the truss
the snarl of a nest, once
a lookout for catching courtship
dives. Lost sight
of weighty forested bends
and sought
more crimson
setting in my periphery.
Hardly housebroken,
how could I fly
all the way to Mexico,
Alaska, the French Foreign Legion's
last outpost? The osprey pair stayed
invariably poised at the lip
of the swamp, where
the spring peepers recanted
their loneliness, asking
where is home? In the slurry
of leave-taking, asking
can we keep it?

Raven on the Watertower

Just when we thought we'd heard
every sound these birds can utter
this one hewed out a burr,
between a reed and a bittern,
the rasping of wheat and the wear
of a rubber belt in the heart
of a machine. Every time
it called the whole body
buckled, became
compound, all beard and sawed
wing feathers: a black
sack of war, weather, dolour.
An alloy of hoarse, crumpled rags.

Was this a thing dying?
Would it have been disingenuous
now to add a second raven,
a companion to ease
our own choking solitude
while cliff swallows like fireworks
divebombed overhead?

A Hyena at the Bodega

There is a curse going on here. Bawdy
and clotted in gusty shadows from the street,
      she squats awkwardly on the chair, twists
her head to forage a bit among her matted clumps of fur.
      She has made sure to step out of her pants
before ambling into view, balled them up. There is a way
      she has of erasing memory; the hackles on
her spine go back a long time. She doesn't even glance
      at the menu. Her dining companion is a good man
if a little uneasy. It is his fault, after all,

      that there's a hyena in the bodega. She paces, totters
on her rusted nails, flicks her hind legs and her ass twitches
      like a double chin. He smokes, waits for it to be over,
tries to see where the rain spots the black road
      blacker. Giving in is easier when there are spots
all over, it smoothes the furious trying to fit
      together. He lowers his voice, can't pretend
he didn't know from the start. She is a supplicant
      slavering at his legs and he continues to smoke.
She cannot keep him. Her eyes are not cavernous enough

      to be interesting, her tongue will be soapy on him. None of us
will keep him for long. Outside, the stars find a clear patch,
      organize themselves into the warped wink
of a stolen path. The other patrons seem unconcerned.
      They have seen all this before. Only a woman
on the other side of the glass presses her hand to the window,
      says silently, *no deberías estar acá*, you should not
be here. Her palm whitens and her old turquoise eyes would seem
      familiar but the window is so dark
and all he can see is his own face: weary, wanting blood.

Conservatory

It was the reach and shudder across the open
    string, the bow a clavicle treacherous
    with memory, that let us believe we had tried
    as hard as we could when we were young to take it
    with us, undistracted by the demands
    of acceleration, the uncertain companionship
    of sorrow and wisdom. The taste of that closed room

    was like old paper, old cologne. The petals had fallen
    from the red roses and the white were brittle
    to be sure, but complete, closed like jilted fists, missing
    the filigreed metacarpals' infinite
    division. The windows threw back no more
    than reflections and we envied their poise.

    Our bodies now are shoddy
metronomes. What still beats
has decided to relinquish belief
in linear time, so we let ourselves go, slur
across the countryside and when we jump fences we land
as we can in our dreams, bionic.
The fields are marked by sharp new furrows

running north and south. In the centre
stands always a tree, for shade and for delight,
and beneath it the cellist. The whole is a study
in madness:
        it is a hundred years ago, we are changing
        the fortunes, allowing
        a damper to drape over the evening,
        over the fields, the hands, the house.

With Arms Outstretched on the Lambton Line

Thirty-six days of thunderstorms
doesn't seem like a great deal. What goes on
the other three hundred and twenty-nine

in London, Ont., the country's capital
for that weather phenomenon? Not much
else in its favour really. Likely

I'll get hate mail for that, from those who prefer
their creeks well paved. In any case, London
is a miscalculation. In fact, the thunderstorms hang out

to the left a little, in a folly
near the Lambton line. You can find it
if you know it's there, and there

are the thunderstorms you seek,
one after another, all close calls with lightning bolts
and crashing, tequila-drunk skies. The rest

of the time? While you wait you can build snow
forts with elaborate moats, you can
practice skulking on the loam

without sinking
in your spooky shoes, try to catch
your peripheral vision

in the act, or take your turn planting
windmills. Mostly those three hundred odd days
will be spent trying to outplay fate,

scarecrow-still and grounded,
hoping this is it, today
could be the day.

On the Eve of Return to Hamelin

On stilts in the metro of a Friday
morning, he plays to no one but the station's
dally: the piper draws us out.

We scatter asunder our cloaks, our half
hearted aubades, and give over our
mourning to play with the station's

indoor birds, blurs of yellow and red
scattered asunder. He wields the half-cloaked
promise of foil balloons, their silver sides

winking light: the piper draws us on.
The tune he plays is not yet invented.
A heart's murmur, it doesn't offer

the name of this mountain,
nor does it pledge return in silver-sided balloons
drawn by birds of red, yellow.

We have chiselled ourselves,
with grief no one wanted,
like fingernails or glaciers over

this mountain we called nameless.
We gnashed our way across jealously,
as if we could claim birds, claim red,

claim yellow. And the piper brings us out
from the mountain he scattered us under.
With his fingers of silver he cracks

the rock where the light gets in and we follow
on stilts from the metro the Friday
on the eve of return to Hamelin.

Prelude to Jumping in the River

He unpeels himself, lays his light shirt, glasses, straw hat
and shoes on the sea-monster
driftwood, where they rest as easily
as they do on him. The mental preparation
takes some time. I have also stood
on that rock, feet cupping
the low, flat lip. The decision is not yet made.

What goes on at the edge of the bank
could last years, centuries. The bottom will shift or
vanish entirely, will push
from the muck we can barely toe
deeply rooted lilies, suckling
bladderwort. Its weight separating it
from the air, the water seeks
itself and stays there, closing
without fuss over whole worlds. It has swallowed
countless resolves to jump or retreat
and kept no record of either. Yet —
the pizzicato of the crickets, the stream — this is at stake,
and it remains enough to give us pause.

The exit, too, will be graceless. There are no footholds
among the reeds and we can barely heave
the body up. We are hopelessly terrestrial, and vaguely,
mnemonically aquatic, but never both at once. In the end,
I catch the aftermath: the slowing ripples, the dogs
rushing down the hill, the surprised head bobbling
above the water. Waiting, I have missed the jump,
the perfect, reckless moment when we cannot turn back.

Talking like Stones in the Night Zoo

You are mistaken, today is not the biting day
but the morning after a night unslept

that leaves us spent while the biter, who is at once
ghost-lover and sweater-pile-destroyer, tumbles through.

That white night's the sort that helps you forget yourself
and the 40 cents owed to the pet shop girl, which feels like bad karma

when all you want is a budgerigar but everyone shakes his head,
assumes you'll trade it for booze. That's how they are. One night

I called a guy a dick for lecturing a homeless man
and he chased me down west 55th shouting, *I am not a dick.*

I'm not a dick! Calling, he didn't know, is a form of love,
its snowy descendent. We give a name — star, ptarmigan,

atomic bomb, in that order — and look at us loving, asway
on the back porch at nightfall. We roar even though what ekes out

chokes on our angry tongues. Yet other days love bows out
in perfect tune, the prelude from Bach's fifth cello suite. Yes

the very one we listened to in lieu of love those nights
when the words were clamped down like the best way to catch a bird.

That promise, the minor key of the American dream — it'll modulate
near the end, it could resolve. It has us by the hairs, filigree

fingering the new flesh underneath the weight
of all that evolution. More efficient to compress the bird

or to club it down from the tree or shoot it
so that it falls easily, as in a winged western,

stumbles from the porch clutching its breast and muttering the name
of its beloved. Before its bloodening eyes are flashes of life,

the three flaws: mistaking good olive oil for bad,
Tchaikovsky for Brahms. What else? That is,

if you're sure you want to catch a bird at all. Otherwise
you're looking like a fool with a limp chip of feathers

the colour of honeydew, a sample for your cellar's decor.
Careful who you pretend to be. Humiliation will show

in the shoulders, the soft watched-out crook
beneath the collarbones that in halcyon days

was so fit for kissing. Faced with incision, we remember the third:
the admission of impotence that is speech while dancing.

We say the words instead of love, keep ourselves revocable,
when we are standing stone-still, blithely confessing our dreams

to the sleeping beasts around us in the night zoo. All waiting
for dawn, for the sky to split open, for stars to dart out

like awkward shorebirds. We're anxious to get started,
set bridges alight. Hang on,

we'll burn them when we get there. Don't be sad.
Today is not the biting day, that's all.

II

II

Preemptive Fieldnotes

> *"Blessed is the one who has arrived at infinite ignorance."*
> — Evagrius Pontus

i.

What if the world is a slide? Weren't we
on our way to pick fruit
heard of in dreams? Let us proceed

with caution. What if
the world is a slide, hurtles
down and us with it while around us slip

all the lucky pennies we have ever found
and all the playing cards? Once
there was a girl who found them wherever

she went, staring at her from sidewalks. A queen,
a two of hearts, the hearts an answer — yes,
certainly — to unspoken questions: is the world

a slide? Asking about love, about what might scare us
more than we'd like, asking about those two guys
who are laughing in front of the house. Is this

my house, my penny, my card, my answer?
Down, down go used batteries, detergents, vulcanized
rubber, bags of sulphate fertilizers. We are a cascade

of wine, dried fruit and fireworks, headed for a facsimile
of south, though the compass rose
knows not to put much stock in direction,

in magnetic north. It wanders, evades
one estimate after another. We have arrived
at falling; where are we falling

from? Dream fruit we dimly
recall as down we domino
with matches, with assorted

barbecues, their carefully stowed coals
puked out black and irregular, like accumulated
debts to criminal organizations, the innards

of dangerous women. Everything
we have ever swallowed cavalcades:
wantonly consumed words

like melon and plant and planet and horse
all so far gone
they've emerged pure again,

dust capsules excreted
from a brimstone-laden universe.
What does brimstone look like? Would we know

if we saw it? Is it reminiscent of
the morning after, cells left
on the pillow? Can we learn

to sleep on this slope? We can learn
anything, to live with the rasp
of gravel from the melting snow.

ii.

For good, winter has receded, drooled
the other seasons in its wake. This
is our salt, the remnants of our oceans

or convivial tides, dregs from a factory
spitting out old men who collect
their cardboard, whose silence is a sign of having

given up. They have relinquished names
and look at us oddly as they somersault,
peddling while they drop. Our stare

is soggier still than the rags they ferry
down. Perhaps they will get pennies for the bundles
they have ribboned for safe-

keeping, like love letters.
At least cardboard insinuates
wall, house; it was once

corrugated around dolls, or metal parts
whose meaning lies in the fabrication
of something larger. When the cardboard is dry,

we can ride on it, slide down
without worries about the sun's febrile reflection.
If there were a roof

it would scatter amoebas
of shade over us and now we find ourselves
craving a roof, a cover. The sun's cauterizing fever

makes us slip faster, want
down before the bottom. It could impel
the wild evanescence of a climb

over the side, little edge that can't claim
to contain or protect. Caution,
remember. We may be on a course as jealous

as a lover and as implacable.
Though we hurry we'll never
reach the voice we can almost hear. Come to me

says the siren in a cardboard house, whispering
in a dream. Oneirism the worst
vice. Sweet or otherwise, our dreams are

of pomegranates mistaken
for power generators, rapid bursts
of movement, fast

as if our skin were made of unsnaggable wool.
This is how we know
it will pick up again. The sun grows

hotter, the sky so blue
I feel almost guilty about it
and now we decide

we will crave
water to precede us down. We buy into
craving like nothing else. The bottom,

we agree as if we were highly trained
mystics, will be soft. When you feel it come
you can get air

as you go over. You may be reminded
at this juncture of a time before you knew
about longing. Tuck your legs

and the last part will be easy. So what
if the world is a slide? Is it
too late already, have you acted on

your unruly impulses? The sun is a mimic
of itself, harbours no sharp regrets
about allowing a few

to get away. It turns its blind eye
to us hoarding the brimstones, pretending
not to.

iii.

You can see for yourself. The heaviest
hearts are the first to go, no matter
what you've heard about bricks

and feathers. What if the world is a slide
and its gentle slope
a misrepresentation? We are tired of dreaming

of gods. We want at least a lack
to pin us. Maybe it's a phase, a prelude
to gentleness, a way of saying I will be

sorry. The concatenation of apologies
will loosen, give way to a veritable fiesta
of atonement, to screams like a thousand lucky

unlucky pennies screeching to the bottom,
their pantomimed shadows thrown
overboard. Gather yourself

and the drop will be light; the sand, a little wet,
will cushion your fall and there you'll be
with all the imaginaries you're ever spoken to,

all the distinctions you've hoped for.
The slide will veer of its own accord
and after the break,

many items of playground apparatus will be stolen
by metal thieves. Coveting will begin
in earnest. The sky's still so blue but clouds

roll in, the yellow of a tornado
coming, of a volcanic moon, molten
and solid at once, of tattoos or decorative inlays

on furniture we can no longer sit on, roped
off at the museum. It leaves us
an indistinct vantage

from which to watch it all slide
down the road, new gas-efficient
coins that mean mostly errands, trips

to the hardware store
where you can get lost in the brimstone
aisle, find what you need to pave

your way to weddings, to the betting pools
of children gathered around a constellation
of marbles. No way they're giving in. They hold

blindness and food in the same fist, neither
edible nor too cold, and fiddle with a note
that reads: a kid in a park halfway across a far-

fetched country is right now
inhaling uranium, becoming
translucent. She sees

through her hand to the impractically green
field, clings imprecisely to each piece
of hoped-for vestige. Only her sadness

is allowed, a wild card to carry
everyone else's. Even the roots of blessing
have to do with blood.

epilogue

No road blocks were erected, just the bodies
of gods who have skidded under
the aluminium, the silvery white healing

over them, leaving
contusions we will have
to fly over. Have we given it

our best shot? I'm scared, that's all. Ascension
is more complex than it seems. Look,
now someone has pressed the secret-agent button

and what stairs were left have eased,
collapsing into zoomed
continuity, from seeing to not

seeing. How did we get here? Look
at all these people calling
to me; how I am loved. Not

every question will be answered. Four
isotopes of sulphur
are stable. The rest, short

lived, expire without explanation. They peter out
with the precision of ripples. Circles work,
it turns out, because squares are too concerned

with themselves, as are the rectangles, though slightly
more willing to stretch. A circle best marks
the spot, it is the best prep

for the attack. As for the rest,
you will be notified by mail.
Is the world a slide? You will be notified.

III

Taking Apart the Harbour

The stars between the rigging are easy to see. The ropes
are taut and it's hard to argue with the steady clang
of the pulleys, the masts that go unequivocally upwards.

An able juggler strolls along this Pythagorean
graveyard. His feet guignol, he flips
to the sky three stars and the harbour doesn't mind.

It too is full of stars, shoved tight between the sailboats
defrocked for the night. It's a matter of finding
his next step, judging what space is empty. He trusts

that tonight it will not rain. Tonight while no one is watching
a derrick will haul its heavy neck over the water
and begin the strike, one slab of steel

at a time, rust and briny patches shaken loose
like blisters. The dislodged hold, the helm,
the walls and floors suddenly alike, all corroded rafts left

to hold aloft another generation.
Lovers one day will sprawl on them oblivious
to the bolts digging at their backs

next to clasping fingers. Bare-chested men will ransack the flats
at low tide for scraps, slice their skin open on the edges
of the flaking red wall left

with a jackladder dangling. The angles
slackened and wound up will hang
on a cloudy cleat. Where the stars come from

is up there; where they fall
will be wolf bait. He knows he'll never
see them land.

Paradise, Dam, North Shore

It prods with its beak
the heaving flanks, lets the fish wait
for death. The heron too waits. Its feet wrap the rock
like gnarled lichen and its breath rises
and ends someplace deep and slow. Desire
is a vertiginous warmth spread slowly;

has it really to do with hunger? I trace
circles on the shale, my scratch
in this ordinary riparian melodrama: the dammed river,
the rapids' patient frenzy, the black-capped night herons
lined up on the shore, poised, eager and pathetic

but the one who gets it is the great grey-blue,
who dips in and spears the carp,
forces the skin apart, slits it like a mouth
before swallowing it whole. There is no forethought
to concupiscence. We are thinking

of paradise, which is not thinking at all.
We like the enfolding conflagration, we like
swallowing it whole. Later I will barely recall
that moment's mindless hunt
as I push against my lover, not telling
of the flat, fat, silvery body
pulsing at the mouth of its captor.

On the floating dock, silvered

Shortly after dawn, all the children walked to the shore, careful
not to rattle lake pebbles with their toes, hoping in the dimness
they might see deer drink. That morning, a bull moose ran
to the edge of the cliff, for a second stopped and looked up,
his cloven hooves small and split on the rocks. He jumped,

legs stuck out in unruly silhouette. We considered burying him
in the sand, finally dragged him to the lake and towed him
to the deepest part. It was over anyway, that year's swinging
on the looped twist of hemp, launching our unbreakable bodies.
We swirled this story around for summers afterwards

like smudges of bitumen, its shifting edges clean.
Death, a daguerreotype quicksilvered stroke after stroke
until it is set. It might have been better to tame the living,
those knots of sharp hunger circling us over the floating dock.
Instead, we waited for the horseflies to land, counted and dove together.

Their geological insect abdomens dithered back and forth,
the prickled, shifting weight exploring like a finger
beneath the hair. Go under, stay to see the shapes air draws
as an afterthought. Beyond the visible depth, there is a graveyard
of gleaming lures, eyes lining the sandy curves, the bed

of dead leaves. Pull towards a rocky archipelago, walk out
on peeling stringy roots. Step carefully, feet white
and unformed in the green water, where you may find
old bottles, shards of ceramics. This far, it becomes difficult to tell
which way the light enters, and which way is down.

When the Ice Breaks

When the ice breaks we will have been in hiding for months,
marvelling, getting fat. The thick panes will rise
like fragmented mausolea shoving each other up and out
of the ground, out of the dark and white underside
of the water. We will watch the river's calving though we have nothing

to do with it. We leave it to chance, peer out
at this lout, the current, tipping burly triangles upside
down over the rapids' drop as the mark rises
higher with each spring day. No earthly thing
can stop this dispersal, nor should we try. A month-

long tyranny has been coiled inside
the undertow all the months
of winter, waiting to be born, to rise
screeching until the whole valley is filled with nothing
but the pestling din of ice on ice, breaking and breaking out.

They will tip off the bridge posts, delicate and surprised,
flip and skim the bottom, clumsy, eager things
obstinately pushing through whirlpools, all sides
and flat planes. In less than a month,
we know, the ice will be dissolving, the water out

in the open. There will be nothing
left but an adjustable wound and out
of these fissures will surge waves, each month
new winds, warmed and lifted slightly with the rise
of the moon. The very idea of stillness will be tossed aside,

left until the later months to arise
from out of the blue, the river thinking of nothing.

Poem for the Sand Verbena Moth

There is no bunchgrass left,
no points of white to make the valleys look taken
aback and so the moth worries

between our window panes, edging
into our house, an itinerary
on its forewings. In the dark

it goes by geomagnetic clues — psst!
The earth is here! — until it finds
our lamp, lands and scuffs the light

into short-lived exclamations
over the dusty stalks. We know
the moth by nighttime and then only

when it tacks up against
the uneven walls, wings flattened
not as an omen, but because it can't be helped.

There is no bunchgrass left
and the moth turns
to screen doors, or lanterns or

the quiet corners where it understands
it is lost and waits tensely
for the death we elaborate for it.

Basin No. 3

Tracing our steps from the railyard, you'd think we were kids
looking for a place to fuck, or graffiti artists intent
on the highest overlooks.

The heavy corrugated door has been crowbarred.
Steps wander down to where grey water would rise
to the waist, concealing corners,
monsters. Metal rungs lead up, many missing,
and the moonlight riffles in, lighthearted,
unconcerned with destruction.
Past the long rooms lined with left-over
tracks; past the central tanneries, their floors covered
in ankle-deep ash; past the pretty windows, the city, the gratification
of having climbed; past the silent passages,
metallic on the tongue as the lower tunnels of a mine —
it's easy to miss the small fuse box
and all its wires ragged.

Here, two pigeons have come to die,
their bodies bundled fatly, breast nestled, as though by art or design,
against breast, and flight is an eddy of old
feathers, brown and unquilled at our feet.

Oversight

Sharp and white, the moon notches the horizon,
funnels clouds into the early morning
hoodlums pushing bicycles through alleyways, past gaping

casements. In the sticky heat, lovers conclude the night naked
and not touching. Fruit, rugs, all-nite coffee storefronts elapse. Perhaps
the day will illuminate new absurdities. The buses are full

of men, their apparatus and tired beards, their metal boxes
shiny between scuffed boots. Everyone gets off, everyone
else gets on. The vanished uncurl from rags and boxes, mute

in brooks of garbage juice. No longer full nor numb,
they throw off blankets on the marble ramparts of insurance
buildings, emerge surprised and maybe a little disappointed

to be not dead. The bus runs a red
and the moon slides down between the towers,
not really bothered, not bothering.

Warm Water Train

Before even the rush of wind, there is the turbid heat
that skims under the skin. Everyone pants
and pushes their backs against the walls,

chins tilted up. If a brazen hand
should brush a hip, the result would be a slow
leaning in. The doors glide together with a muffled breath

and an old woman dabs herself with the ropes of her scarf,
runs it on her neck, slips it between
her breasts to sop up the sweat suspended there.

Someone offers her his seat, hooks his coat over the chrome,
fanning himself with a paperback of *La Peste*.
He chafes his tie loose, unbuttons his shirt

with three fingers, flaps it like a sail around his paleness.
At the back of the car, a boy and a girl speak
in sign language. He is warm, the boy grumbles,

knuckles essing the air, hot under the collar.
She agrees and in silence they step out
of their shoes, socks. Water streams over their feet,

warps the speckled linoleum into silvery minnows.
The girl unfolds her dress over her head, kneels in the puddle
and bathes her face. The underground is always this hot, and now

the Camus reader is shuffling from his trousers, lurching
as the cars lurch around the bend and bawl to a stop
halfway in the dark tunnel. Like peeling leather

gloves one finger at a time, yanking with the teeth
to wrench the hands free, everyone takes off his clothes.
A yellow dog sags her head between her paws,

her withers low towards the heart. Her lupine eyes
consider the spills charting out across the floor, wait
for the train to fill up. The old woman

wrings out her scarf. She is undressed
and her olive skin glistens. In the dimming light,
she braces herself against the vinyl wall,

sinks under the surface. Only
her shoulders and head are visible,
and finally the whole body is below.

Ship in a Bottle

There are inlets, discovered on canoe trips
and childhood stomps, that lend themselves to long days
and elaborate laic baptisms. Their names are invented to scare

our younger selves: the one we called Cemetery
Bay, in the north corner of Kashwakamak, where the afternoon
shivered the boat in shadow; a creek on the Magaguadavic

where that cormorant stretched, its orange beak distending sun.
They go as far as we want them to, show us bark etched
with an old man's inscrutable face, pine roots climbing

into masts, unfurling in alien directions. Here, in our ship in a bottle,
our fingers are spidery and dexterous, rigging our canoe into
outer space, into a memory we have not yet

assigned. The stripped keel rips
to tip us beneath the viscous green water. We dive shallow,
propelled through the tassels of oarweed, our skinny

torsos writhe through the stained-glass membrane and we are brought
back to what is there to be discovered — a reliquary
of trees, petrified by time and thick water.

The Rough Guide to Home

After the flats of Utah we discovered
we are forest people, trailed the animal
groans for any body of water, unlike
the crazy Texans in long pants roughing it
in their bus, its brassy gasps thriving
and the generator lowing all day long. Sand
was a wry interruption
of barren, the land's language

for itself. I was itched by scurrying
desert gnats, scrutinized
by a conspiracy of ravens chittering
on the ledge, birds big as souls.
Splayed on steaming stone,
embanked by rustling low sagebrush,

we waited for the caprice of night. I understand
three sweatshirts in July, prefer
to shiver bundled and curled
on pink-bellied granite. Give me
blackflies, the shushing congregations
of white pines pitched on an island daubed
by wildflowers along all the rivers,
the logging roads young scars. I walk easily
through creeks. The shallows distort

my feet until they are familiar.
Wild thyme all over and home
is any general store, a trickle

of bait and tackle shops, greens
like homonyms. I will watch the pines lumber
until they are impenetrable, impossible to tell
from their dentition. Then dawn, a yellow lace, forgotten
by those who have gone to be old elsewhere.

Manifesto for August

She was the kind of woman who walks down
Yonge Street on her hands, from far away as Thunder
Bay or wherever it ends — some drive-in

at the edge of the map's frayed wingspan —
drawing downpours all the way. I am
not from here, she sing-songed as the wind slugged

porches from woodslatted houses, freeing
them to drift like continents. Who needs porches
anyway, battering like eyelashes?

The blustery dusk lifted furrowfuls
of seeds with one crooked forearm and flung
them akimbo, where they would sprout, after

many years, perfect, identical fruit.
Just like a woman, this weather system,
the locals asserted crossly. The witch

is in. But I decline, she sniped, to be
cradled or photographed. And took the path
down the hill, into the countryside's

swathed mist, matching her stride to the rhythm
of late sunspots. The roads were lined with gasps
of clover about to get wistful because it never failed,

their luck never turned. Weaving across
she was orange cats, come to take
a stand, she was clowns on a bicycle

until they fall. Her skirt was the fabric
of absurdly coloured apples
and on her head a fuzzy wool cap hid

tale-telling hair. All she wanted now was
a man to scratch up against, peals
of a deeper voice to lap at her. She still got

hot. There was mister July, mister Right
Now, two months too late. She ought to stick
to the deal, half the year in, out, listen

to her mum, but even fertility
symbols — especially fertility
symbols — wore push-up bras. Eros

and Thanatos had gone to the mall
to buy a pet bee so why shouldn't she be the one
to seek him, one gale after another.

Meanwhile the locals were shouting their woes:
so sorry, we weren't careful what we wished
for. Why are there no branches of heavy, saucy fruit

falling on us, why isn't the world beginning
to smell a little bit more
like oblivion? If you don't know

where you're going, there is
a chance you won't get there and sure enough
they fell in love. She came to know

his sure, broad summer's body, the thick
way he loved her. They did it
earnestly, built a cabin in the woods

and adorned it but she couldn't find sense
in essential shelter. She was the kind
of woman who releases bugs by cupped

hand when they're trapped between glass and glass,
offers a hint of darkness in that scorching,
inviting light. She opened the windows and flew out

dotting the air with flotsam: moving,
moving south. Yeah, she missed him. Every boy
was her sweet radio DJ, every

eighties' song was meant for her. Get over it,
her mother told her. It's not like you can
turn your back on mother nature. In time

she went to town, joined the music hall tour,
learned to spin a number of theories
on her snout and received accolades

as the most believable thing to mark
the circuit in years. Wrote a bestseller,
launched a thousand ships, a line of perfume.

Flopped, found herself washing dishes
for a slob in an unholy slum. She grew
beautifully plump. The shorter

the days became, the bigger she got until
she could cover the entire span
of the baseball diamond. Though she'd been

a bit of an ass-kicker, she allowed
herself to be slid between the two storm
proof panes, set to the slog of winter's work:

remembering birds of paradise, knitting
them sweaters to unravel come spring.
How would it end? Only the same, the same.

Song of my Old Lead Pipes

Our toilet bellowed as the water purred unevenly
through the pipes, its song spiralled in the throat,
the elbow. At first we thought we might repair it,

but it would have meant ripping the entire house
from its waist, lizarding more cracks
through the tired walls starting to get used

to the shift from the ice storm years ago.
So we found other tones to go with it, composed
arpeggios to the plumbing's deep bass drone. We arranged

our lips like thick jazz trumpets, looped the descant
of our giggles and let loose inchoate streams
of scah hah tat dah doo dah dah doo — . Finally

I called a friend who had a piano but didn't play
and I hummed the toilet note into the phone
until my gums were numb. I hummed and he plunked

from the right though in the end
we never could find what it was — B, B flat
below middle C — that our pipes were piping.

Ladder to the Middle

The ladder, perplexed at the utility that calls it out into the disquiet
of the work lights on the empty stage, draws down

the corners of its mouth, stops with hands on its hips, feet apart.
But for an invitation, it could dispense invaluable advice, rules

for the way we move: to be edgy, use your elbows more. It dies
a little in indecision and prefers, artlessly, to leave the fold and fall

to others. In any case, there's really no changing its mind.
Once the climb and tinkering are complete — and the descent too,

it wouldn't do to leave a man marooned
in mid-air — it will be relegated to toy boxes, dreams

and the forms of angels. It knows about luck,
shabby English stockings, obsolete elevators. But it stands

for the victory of geometry, and only wants
to get closer to god, to bring us there.

IV

Barometer

The trouble with deciding to kiss someone,
anyone, anywhere at all — the hand, or at the foot

of a canyon — is that the moment you lean
over, mean to displace the air

between mouth and mouth and hover
at the bottom of that canyon, so far

below sea level there is no question
that perception is screwed up

and we might as well be speaking
German for all the good the kiss is doing,

that instant as you linger for some display
of intention and get an inkling

it's the pressure that holds it
together, the moment you give

in and the jig is up and the cat
is out happens precisely

when the beloved aspires
to be wholly other, spots the twin boomerangs

of swifts mating on the wing,
is when the river decides

to peruse the craggy landscape, embark
on its mid-afternoon drench, slaloming against the walls

even burros can't scale and slams beneath
the nearly kissing, sweeping

them off their feet, to somewhere or
else.

Life Jacket

Out of the bright middle of the night like a lunatic
I wanted to hike out waving my life jacket (the method
of sorrow) until a Native guy on the Faro road stopped
in his pickup — "Excuse me sir, do you have a phone?
I've had a premonition." I have seen your body seize,

your eyes seared and blue drinking in the sky while in mine
the sun never sets these days. I am nowhere
on this river, wish you were here, and not stranded
at the mailbox. I can't tell if the red flag is up
but animals are going nuts all around you in your night garden —

the marsh hawk raucous, the wasps, the crickets roaring
like dusty know-it-alls — as you set about returning
my blank postcards with their old-looking
snapshots of paddlewheelers on a river
that is fast, but not as fast as it looks. To say what?

Take care, all my men die in dreams these days.
Back in the boat; it will end as it should,
and I don't know how to make it otherwise. To say, oh
come. I will be at the road, life jacket in hand. You can't miss me,
I'm the one trying this time not to look back.

Strawberry Jam

It trickles slowly, like a scowl, like patience or mockery, layers
of congealing fruit winding in languid coils in the bottom

of hot Mason jars. The felt-tipped date recalls slapped-open
doors and windows, my shirt stuck to my chest in dark ovals.

Even the birds were silent in that heat. In the kitchen,
my mother and I continued to stir strawberries into pulp. My pot

is not nearly as big as hers, huge and red and painted
with white flowers, deep enough to bathe a baby in.

It belonged to our neighbour, an old woman whose decrepit
yellow house was the fancy and fright of all of us growing up.

When she died, the lawyer dragged her accumulated
possessions to the edge of the road, where they hunched,

ill at ease, blinking in the unexpected sunlight.
My mother eyed the pot for days. It sat complacent

on the green velour of a parlour chair. There were lamps
everywhere. When my mother went into the street

that evening to retrieve the coveted pot, a tall black torchère
fell backwards, metal shade tilted, the bulb bursting

with a surprising lightness. Leaning
the lamp in the crook of her elbow, both hands claiming

the pot, my mother, torn between embarrassment
and some sense of art, fumbled to restore the heap.

The lamp and my mother, at the end of the way,
silhouetted, two crazy women suddenly unsure

whether they'd been asked over. Yesterday morning I tilted
the end of one jam jar into the beginning of another, trying to tell

when empty is empty, though the deep red stickiness lines
each raised glass letter, as if the jar had been blown in the same

flames that make our summer kitchens untenable, in what stays
though we decide we are done pouring.

En promenant ma peine d'amour

It drags me along, hauls at the string
with which I try to restrain the worst impulses:
never calls, doesn't bring flowers, eats
diapers out of other people's garbage. I follow
its disappearance and wonder what in its nature makes it escape
me? See how I am tangled in the junipers,
those brown sheep eyes bay, eloquent
in the silent swindle that is their specialty.
No one's fed me in months, I remain underpetted, forbidden
to chase anything. Poor thing, though as ever
it is me who walks into the thicket, not the other way
around, who pries out (tenderness
incarnate) the quills of that audacious adversary.

But we are the foolhardy here, launching into
that obvious ambush every time, and we are left,
the beast and I, at work with forceps, coaxing out
the barbs. Short memory, this one;
before long the sizeable hobo is back
on the tracks, its dogged refusal
to leave alone the tall and dark
until I shrill Drop it! Drop it!
which of course it disregards.
Does it really know better than me
where we want to go? Here's the deal: no climbing
on the bed, monthly baths at least, no inordinate fascination
with other people's ankles. Okay, some
climbing on the bed. Otherwise — I threaten the gag,
the heeling, the embargo on treats —
I'll hitch it to a sled, just keep moving on.

Crash Cymbal

Charles Mingus was dubbed
a sex pervert when they discovered him
pouring hot sand down the front of his trousers
because it felt good. I remember

when you said you'd love me forever
because I smoked like a trucker
out the side of my mouth, my hands
full of instruments. That same day I dropped
your crash cymbal on the concrete floor

and it felt good, while the Indians played chess
at the end of the loading dock
and didn't even look up at the clamour.
I saw it go, anticipated the gong:
baroque, enormous. It teetered
on its circumference

faster, and faster still like crickets
going mad until the stillness
that means, I have fallen, the edge
has caught. I waited

for the sand to pour
from the heavens, from the roof
where Mingus, exhausted from love,
proposed. His father claimed
insanity ran in the family,

and he was underage
by several years, still playing
sharp, hoping to get old

before his time. None of us
has got it yet, but when we find it
we'll play that damn note every single night.

The Time of Figs

To tell if a fig is ripe and good to eat,
wrap your hand over its folds and press
into the eye. If it gives, drips a circle

in your palm and along the ridge
of your thumb, its pliant heart is ready
to be husked apart.

                We often tell
of a trip my father took, after the wars
had ebbed enough to allow a path

through the sinews of the Biokovo, escape
in reverse. His brother had driven up, waited
in that dim cleft between childhood

and return. In the din of the airport,
they acknowledged each other, unsure
and suspended. The dilapidated German car

honked into each mountain bend, tracing
an earlier flight, when a younger man had left
his siblings crouched by the woodpile.

Face pressed against the window,
my father stared over the amber faults
of the precipice, angled sharp

and sloping out. The road curved
like the outline of a hand, shallow print
of twenty years away.

     The fig is a flower,
inverted as if peering to see inside
its own skin. Impatient, the pulp begins to dry

still on the tree, aloof and folded. The laden branches
drape low, reach for their roots and the husk gathers
like a minaret.

     By the mouth of the Neretva,
they saw fig trees by the road, and leaves,
curled, creased and withered

by the week-long sleet storms
that ended the drought. The splintered earth
was covered with the flattened rosettes of figs.

In the heat that summer, my grandmother
stayed bedridden in the little house. She counted
her breaths, tracked the pace of her heart and watched

the vines grow heavy, parched and yellow.
After the rains, the ground was stained
with the mottled bruises of fruit.

        The fig
seems to open in slow motion, divulging
of its own accord an entire world

rattling in its veins. It unfurls like a lantern,
splattering light, the pink flesh clasping
the stippling of seeds.

     My father and his brother
stopped at the slatted stand of a man selling pears,
pomegranates, and honey — jarred pollen of such thick gold

they could see the filaments of sugar.
Through the glass, the sun ricocheted
the field-dances of springtime bees.

It was late September and the figs were cheap,
thirty kuna a kilo. We'll take them all, they said, complicit
again, and by the time they arrived at the church,

the rusted cistern, the stone house,
my father and my uncle had eaten all five kilos.
This is how we tell it. There were fingerprints

of juice on the steering wheel, on my uncle's slacks
and down my father's forearms, the rivulets drawing
and re-drawing maps on his skin.

Sun Days

Could be a trick of the light,
of the long dusk that isn't:
sleep, love, the snows that stay put
and entreat us to run them down the side of mountains
from where we began, well past the treeline.

Well past a reasonable time to keep hoping
for sleep, love, I pack a bag with apples, with darkness
to release later, head towards
the north, places that are cut more clearly
even as the roads make less sense.

Less sensible than other ways of gathering
sleep, love, and the wood we'll need to get us through
the winter, this pursuit will bring me back
where I began, but for now the shadows are so drawn out
they could sleep through any trick, even love.

Errand

I went into the evening
to get plums and
ginger. It seemed suddenly
important and I walked

through the drifts and wafting
snow, the streets quiet but for cars
mewling their wheels and the whistle
of a Vietnamese cook in the alley —

>   was it the ginger
>   for your tea, my love, sick in bed, or
>   was it the blizzard, churlish
>   and stark, its redundant explanations?

— and finally
through the park with my plums,
the ice under me so thick
and so cold.

Silk Pouch Hardware

               Brick by brick
in the brook and living
room — there was a swimming pool
ladder for climbing out
of that turquoise saloon — we stacked one rung
after another. Right away without keeping
track we put up bits of clothing, pearls,
tobacco, flowers. Hard to stack but of course
strangely beautiful as a whooped no-strings mating call
or a look of recognition when we concede beauty,
accept it in lieu of truth. All this exchanged, given
with care once a year or as needed, not strewn
into a histrionic landscape on moors
that tried too hard to be romantic,
couldn't get out of that last century.

               See how long
the road goes on, see this tower for broiling
intergalactic messages. We will
design a time factory,
more reasonably-sized concepts,
a photo booth, a really colourful giraffe.
I know you would tie her shoes
since she can't bend down, scale
her neck to festoon her with streamers.
I know she would trust you utterly.

               Maybe we can take
her picture too, tuck our questions
in the booth's money slot and wait for the kisses
to tumble our way. Snapshot in four minutes

or the giraffe goes free,
gets taller, more colourful.

          On a piano bench
deep underground, we picked
some good notes — a few from
my childhood, from yours — hopped
scotch around the cracks in the sound
board, using for a stone the pit
from the best fruit ever. This is the song
I remember most, an old wuthering
tune so drunk it needs to be carried
around in a silk pouch. You can trade it
if you need to in your travels
for beans, gold
shoes, ointment for old nightmares,
or a new gong. Sound it
and at once you'll be surrounded
by thousands of sleeves
to rest your heart on.

Last Tango in Outremont

Not here the abrupt buttery seduction of strangers.
In these ritardando moments, we are so certain
of what's coming, when the double bass grinds away,
such a good listener, and the violin shrieks —
it can't help it, flicks the inside
of the dancers' skin with its raspy bow.
We crash through the familiar
as through a curtain, cigarette in hand,
finally near someone we've been holding all along.

Three minutes we begin counting
from the first embrace, a figure twined, seamless
even as we chase each other from the Mile End
to the milongas' hysterical time. The inexplicable staccato
pivots, going one way and then the other,
but you can't play a piece of music
backwards, so we dance home, gypsies
with our shoes hooked in our thumbs,

bodies made obvious by the tango
though we hardly know it yet. Our eyes stay closed all night
as the bandoneón swoons, causes the heart
to feel like a walnut in all the best ways, as if to say
will you come to Buenos Aires with me?
We could be big stars, good listeners.

Utensils after the Inquisition

Even the immigration laws
rely heavily on the cutlery drawer.
"Where were the spoons kept?"
they set us apart to ask, but
I could only recall the sharp-edged
hybrid device meant for grapefruit, for hacking
its skins away like no spoon I've ever seen and
you said *basta, basta* and threw a fit.
We don't use spoons, you said,
we slur it all over each other, yoghurt
behind the knees and berries of all sorts
balanced on each vertebra.
"Do you lick each other?"
they asked, fascinated. Yes. We lick each other
from top to bottom.

For years I would be
the charlotte for your teaspoon, rapt
at you curled asleep like a question mark, a smaller
inquisition. Alas, though a thin wedge
of porcelain may know a great deal about rest,
it does not crave, nor suffer.

Never More Temperate

How beautiful our children would have been,
though poor at pool. We could have built with them
delightful offensives, taught them the seduction

of a low voice, they our mouths painted
a sultry, old-movie red and led us,
beautiful as children with early nostalgia,
to now, feeding coins into the evening.

Others may have the body, but we were first
and free from the first uncovering, the young bother
of hearts in the syrup of suburbs. And so remain,
in this guileless, suspended test of tipping off

our ashes, laying unsteady statues of them
for blackbirds to undo. You'd forgotten
half my name and I your favourite colour
of sky. This game might have begun years ago

or it did and we've kept our children
waiting around for us to discover
the snappish beauty in regret,
that patient carnivorous flower.

We could have been doing this already, sinking
like teeth, skidding across the beer-daubed felt
not calling shots, not calling anything.

Love Song for the End of the World

Don't worry, this is a poem
entirely without grace. Instead we will conceive
together of the possible ways
to end the world. Since we have managed
to make even fission
banal, let me design something like
scorpions, like vociferating recklessly
into a sandstorm, or like the sudden discovery
that a mole on your hip
is a detonator. Let us have
all of our fingers cut off, be disfigured
by acid and thrown into a pigpen
in the manner of just so many concubines;
let us be the victims of the flailing
of our limbs against our limbs,
until we tire of the carnage and walk away.
Let us die of mange, of blues guitar, of very bad puns.
Whatever I invent will never be worse
or more spectacular than the dark,
where our bodies should be left at angles, graceless,
though with perspective
the whole pile of us could be read
like tea leaves in an inverted china cup.

If I dreamed your death
it would be in a great wind (nothing
like what you have feared)
and you would swing out like a crane
over the world, grow a skin of feathers and go
to ashes —

To take away, or be slowly taken

At the risk of falling
backwards, craned and shielding our eyes, we sought the polar delicacy
of the birds' underparts, took the shades and spread them,
the contours stannic and garbled. There was something natural

about it. To dry we perched them on a jasmine tree
we'd never known, though it had overtones of a long-standing
contagion. We painted blue what windows we had
and there we made our bed impiously

in the midst of a rubbled house in the city.
The rain was so thick it altered mornings
when they came, as though milk were pouring down.
When they retiled the streets the cobbles went crooked,

and it teemed milky through the roof breached open
to this day, washed through the kitchen and out
into the lane. It has been raining forever and here I am
burning to try to put it out. I don't want to count my days

only to know they exist, and then what? Watch them wash away
with everything else, the lesser betrayals. I revert
to that night, closer to its ancient glittering eye, when I tried
to resuscitate the dark's ancestral smell.

Already the heat was leaching and above us, fixed and
white with wings arced, a tern gone berserk with sorrow,
immobile as myth. We watched the flocks vee south, bring back
the sealed surprise of their noise, their late-night noise. Your eyes

had in them winter and it is so deep, that season
like a tired woman. How easily dispelled my theories

to do with home. That singing around the house was sweet
as butter, as milk claimed by no one, souring. Let's go skip stones

on the flood. If we'd allowed
souvenirs, this is what I would have sent:
ten stones, flat, wide and perfect, angles dulled to blend
into the horizon, to disappear into what could very well be

an infinity in petitions. We learned at our peril what seeps out
each time. We should have been waking elsewhere, instead grappled
unnaturally together to the sky's unbruising. Between us,
a good temptation in the blueing light.

Legs twitching helplessly, it is shelled, glabrous and shy in the breaking
of day. Should we have given it a burial below the jasmine,
or let it stutter overturned while the two of us stood together
as if we had planned to gather here, count the stars as they flashed,

vanished. What sinister optimism. There is nothing small about it.
We will know seasons, other climes. The sun will rise
though we won't see its organza limbs hatching. Go back under, to bed,
to bed. The second time it will be a quiet insistence

after the afternoon storm we have grown to depend on, improvident
but not unaccustomed. Like this fascination with the dawn
as we wonder, what is it we're forgetting, what are we running
out of?

Notes

Some of these poems have appeared, often in other incarnations, in the chapbook *Barometer* (Delirium Press, 2005), on the Poet Laureate's website, in *The Antigonish Review, Contemporary Verse2, echolocation, The Fiddlehead, Grain Magazine, The Nashwaak Review, The Saranac Review, The Spoon River Poetry Review* and *Taddle Creek*.

The author would like to extend her thanks to her editors, to Karen Solie, Barry Dempster, Stephanie Bolster, and Ross Leckie, to others who have shifted the shapes of these poems, to Vinko Grubišić for the spark, to the Conseil des arts et des lettres du Québec, the Canada Council for the Arts and the Banff Centre for their financial support, and to those who gave me homes during the writing and editing of this book.

This book is dedicated to my mother.